IT'S TIME TO EAT ASPARAGUS

It's Time to Eat ASPARAGUS

Walter the Educator

Silent King Books
A WhichHead Entertainment Imprint

Copyright © 2024 by Walter the Educator

All rights reserved. No part of this book may be reproduced in any manner whatsoever without written per- mission except in the case of brief quotations embodied in critical articles and reviews.

First Printing, 2024

Disclaimer

This book is a literary work; the story is not about specific persons, locations, situations, and/or circumstances unless mentioned in a historical context. Any resemblance to real persons, locations, situations, and/or circumstances is coincidental. This book is for entertainment and informational purposes only. The author and publisher offer this information without warranties expressed or implied. No matter the grounds, neither the author nor the publisher will be accountable for any losses, injuries, or other damages caused by the reader's use of this book. The use of this book acknowledges an understanding and acceptance of this disclaimer.

It's Time to Eat ASPARAGUS is a collectible early learning book by Walter the Educator suitable for all ages belonging to Walter the Educator's Time to Eat Book Series. Collect more books at WaltertheEducator.com

USE THE EXTRA SPACE TO TAKE NOTES AND DOCUMENT YOUR MEMORIES

ASPARAGUS

It's asparagus time, let's shout, "Hooray!"

It's Time to Eat
Asparagus

Those green stalks are fresh and ready today!

In the garden or on the plate,

It's the veggie we've been waiting to taste!

Long and skinny, with tips so neat,

Asparagus is a veggie treat.

We wash it, snap it, watch it steam,

Turning bright green, like a tasty dream!

Chomp, chomp, crunch! It's fun to eat,

With butter or cheese, a salty treat.

It's healthy too, from the tip to the end,

Asparagus is our veggie friend!

Grown in fields with the sun so bright,

It pokes through the soil, reaching light.

Spring is the time it loves to grow,

Then off to the market it goes to show!

It's Time to Eat
Asparagus

So when it's time for lunch or dinner,

Asparagus makes you a winner!

Try it roasted, grilled, or steamed,

It's the tastiest veggie you've ever dreamed!

With vitamins and fiber too,

It helps us grow strong, just like you!

Each little stalk is packed with might,

Helping us jump, run, and play all night!

Green like grass or a big tall tree,

It's a super snack, don't you agree?

Dip it, crunch it, have a taste,

No bite of asparagus goes to waste!

Sometimes it's purple, sometimes it's green,

Tall and tasty, like a springtime queen!

No two stalks are quite the same,

.

But every bite's a veggie game!

Pick it fresh or have it canned,

Asparagus tastes great in your hand.

In soups or salads, on your plate,

It's Time to Eat
Asparagus

It's a veggie you'll love to celebrate!

So let's all cheer, let's all say,

"Asparagus time, hooray, hooray!"

Eating veggies is fun, so let's begin,

With asparagus smiles and green-grin grins!

ABOUT THE CREATOR

Walter the Educator is one of the pseudonyms for Walter Anderson. Formally educated in Chemistry, Business, and Education, he is an educator, an author, a diverse entrepreneur, and he is the son of a disabled war veteran. "Walter the Educator" shares his time between educating and creating. He holds interests and owns several creative projects that entertain, enlighten, enhance, and educate, hoping to inspire and motivate you. Follow, find new works, and stay up to date with Walter the Educator™

at WaltertheEducator.com

Milton Keynes UK
Ingram Content Group UK Ltd.
UKHW020821141124
451205UK00012B/659